EVERYTHING YOU NEED TO KNOW ABOUT DINOSAURS

AND OTHER ANCIENT GIANTS OF AUSTRALIA

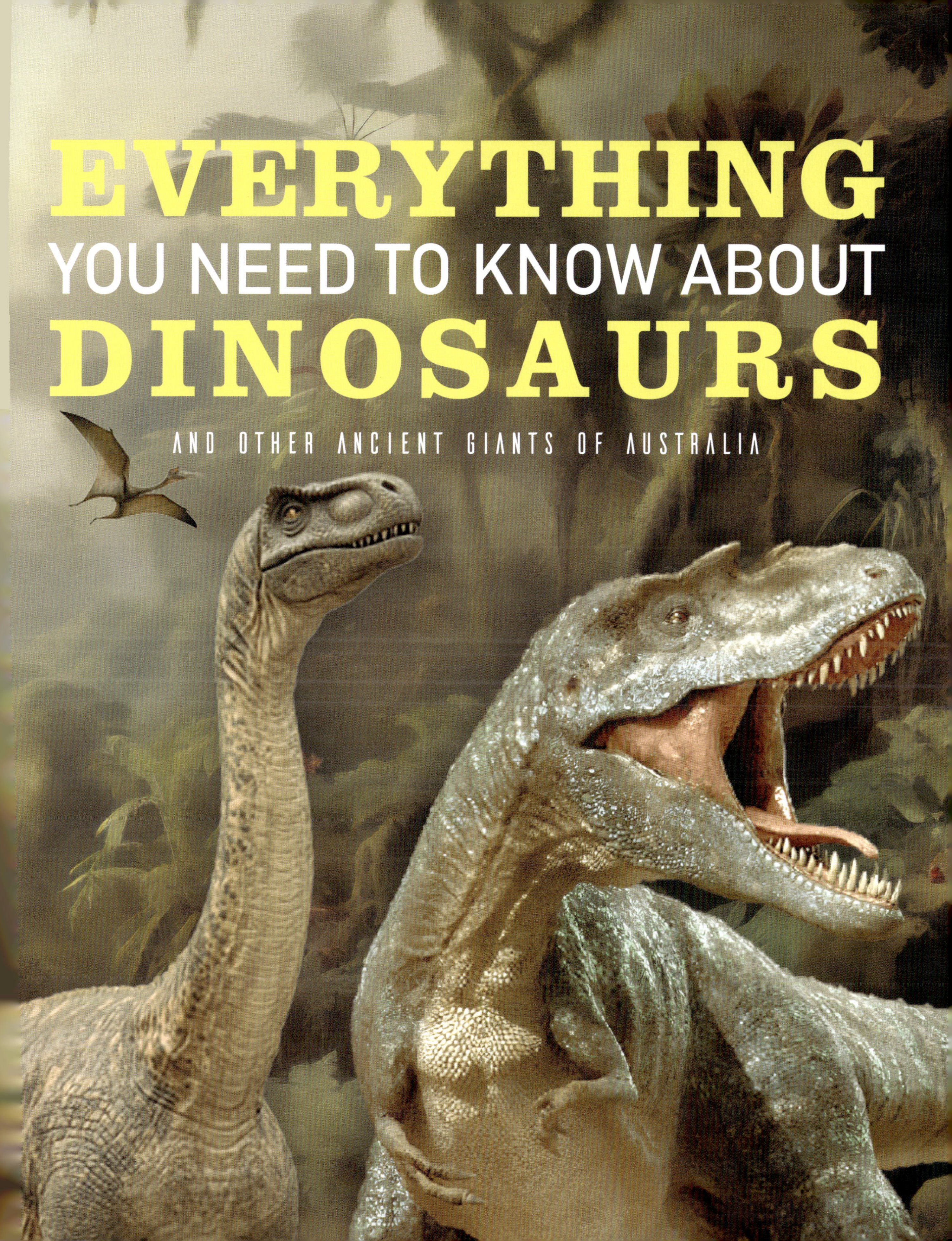

I am very grateful to vertebrate paleontologists Mike Archer, Sue Hand and Trevor Worthy for their time and comments on this book. I also sincerely thank all the people who have provided photographs. I am indebted to you all.

Jenny Jones

This edition published by Young Reed NH in 2025

A record of this book is held at the National Library of Australia.

ISBN 9781921073991

Managing Director: Fiona Schultz
General Manager/Publisher: Olga Dementiev
Designer: Andrew Davies
Production Director: Arlene Gippert
Printed in China

Keep up with New Holland Publishers:
newhollandpublishers.com

Note:
The names of the main animals shown in this book are in **bold**, as are words included in the glossary.
Scientific names are in *italics*, or **bold** within a caption.

Picture Credits
Abbreviations: t = top, b = bottom, c = centre, l = left, r = right, bg = background

Photographs
Aaron Camens: p. 42bl.
Australian Museum: pp. 20br; 21r
Ben Kear (SAM): pp.18; 19c, b.
Brett Robinson: p. 10b.
Elephant Bird p. 33: From Memoires de l'Academie **Malgache**, 1933, Fasc. XV11 Mullerorins, Plate 3.
Fritz Geiser: p. 24br (egg).
Guillaume Louys: p. 28t.
Henk Godthelp: p. 35b.
Illustration in John Gould's The Mammals of Australia: p. 31b.
Jenny Jones: pp. 12bl; 26–27bg; 43b.
Jenny Worthy: pp. 9r; 12.
Jim Gehling (SAM): pp. 8b; 10l; 38b.
John fields: p. 20cr.
John Long: p. 14bl.
Ken Griffiths: pp. 22t; 24bl; 25b; 27b; 28b; 37c.
Lee K. Curtis: p. 43bl.
Mark Hutchinson: p. 9r.
Mike Archer: pp. 31c; 33t.
Mike Caldwell: p. 19tr.
National Archives of Australia A6180, 21/8/78/15: p. 31t.
New Holland Image Library: pp. 2–3 (with Raoul Slater); 8–9bg; 10–11bg; 18–19bg; 20-21bg; 22–23bg; 24–25bg; 24bc; 28–29bg; 34–35bg; 42–43bg.
Queensland Museum: front cover bl & c; pp. 1 b & c; 3bl & c; 7t; 14t; 15t, c, b; 16–17; 36.
Raoul Slater: pp. 1bg; 2–3 (with NHIL); 12–13bg; 30–31bg; 44–45bg; 46–47bg; 48bg.
Rod Morris: p. 40–41bg.
Stephen Jaquiery: p. 7b.
Steve Bourne: cover tr; pp. 3tr; 17c; 35t; 36b; 40bl, br.
Sue Hand: pp. 21tl & tr; 37t;
Themo Terzis: pp. 6–7bg; 14–15bg; 16–17bg; 36–37bg;
Trevor Worthy: pp.3bg; 6b; 7c; 9r; 32; 33b; 32–33bg; 35bc; 38–39bg; 39b; 40tl; 41t; 43t.

Illustrations
Anne Musser: front cover br; pp. 3br; 29b.
Brian Choo: p. 13c.
James Reece: p. 21b.
Josh Lee: pp. 10–11, 23 (jigsaw pieces); 13tr; 39.
Peter Murray: pp. 9tr; 35c; 42t.
Zoë Archer: pp. 9r; 20l; 21t.

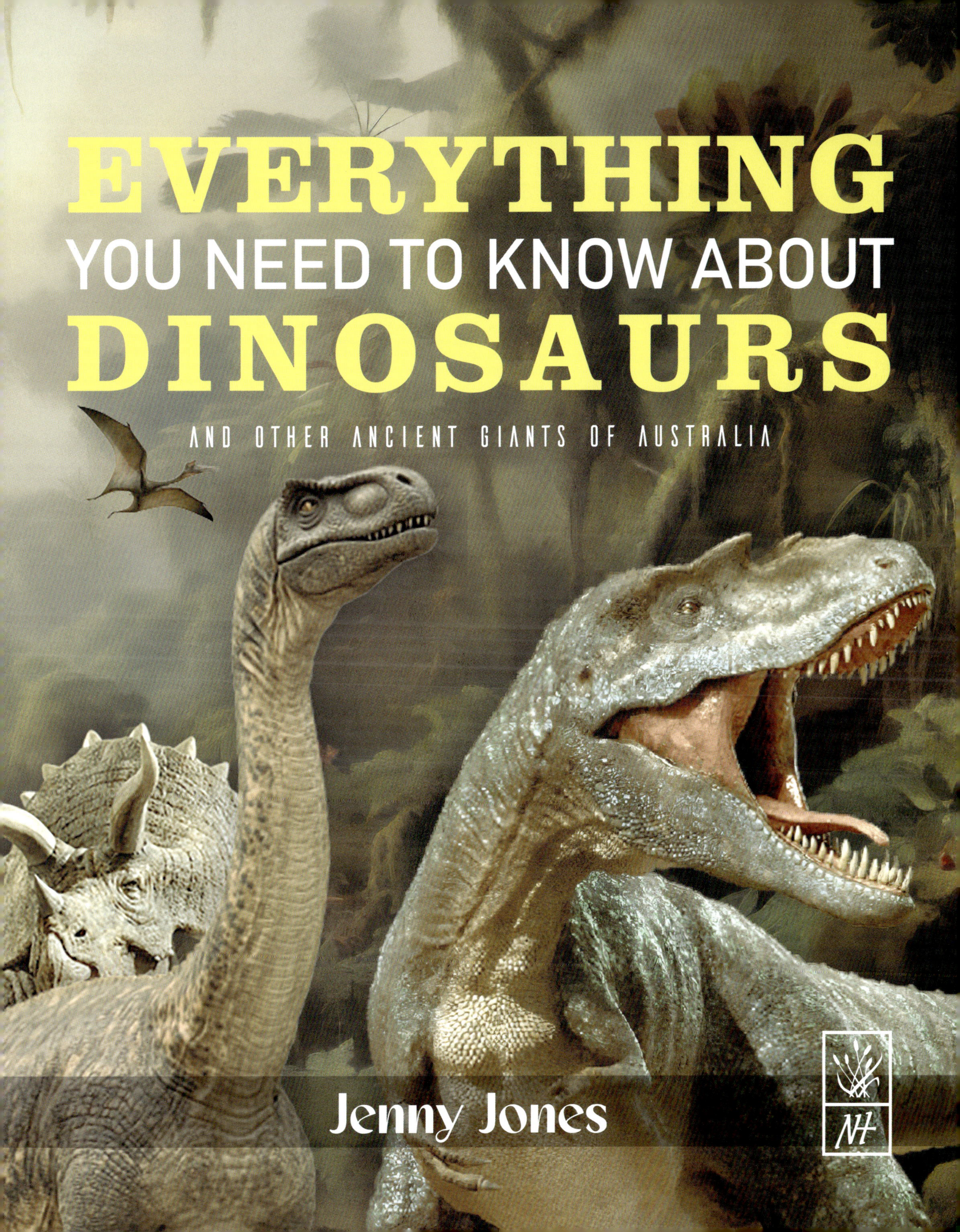
EVERYTHING
YOU NEED TO KNOW ABOUT
DINOSAURS
AND OTHER ANCIENT GIANTS OF AUSTRALIA
Jenny Jones
NH

Important Fossil Sites in Australia

Contents

Prehistoric Australia

Australia is an exciting time capsule—in its soil and rocks **palaeontologists** have found the remains of animals from before, during and after the dinosaurs walked the planet. There are **fossils** from the very beginning of animal life! Some of the most incredible, weird and unique animals have lived in Australia. There are not many places in the world where you can see the **evolution** of **prehistoric** life as clearly as here. Not only did animal life evolve, but so did Australia. It went from being a small part of a huge land mass, called **Gondwana**, to the large separate land that we have today.

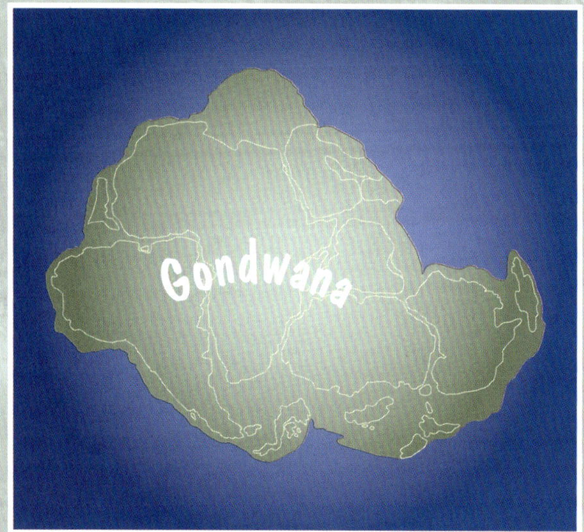

Can you see which sections of Gondwana became which continents when Gondwana broke up? Look on page 47 to see if you were right.

The Gondwana Jigsaw Puzzle

The countries on Earth were not always as they are today. Millions of years ago, there was only one piece of land, which we call Pangaea. About 180 million years ago, this land broke into two 'supercontinents'—one in the north of the planet, called Laurasia, and one in the south, called Gondwana. Gondwana was like a gigantic jigsaw puzzle made up of the lands we now call Africa, Madagascar, India, South America, New Zealand, Antarctica and Australia. Gondwana started to break up into the separate land areas of today about 120 million years ago, with the last separations 40–35 million years ago.

Plant Life on Gondwana

Plants, like animals, started out in the water. The first plants were green, slimy algae. But during the Carboniferous period, from 359 to 299 million years ago, Gondwana was cloaked in green forests. Simple plants like mosses and ferns grew on the ground and tall tree ferns grew with conifers such as the Wollemi pine and kauri trees, cycads and ginkgoes. There were no flowering plants until closer to dinosaur **extinction**.

Non-flowering plants like this cycad were common on Gondwana during the time of the dinosaurs.

Animal Life on Gondwana

Although dinosaurs dominated the Earth for a long time (more than 180 million years!), other animals shared it with them (and came before and after them). There were fish, **amphibians** and other **reptiles**, and the first small **mammals** and birds had **evolved**. But dinosaurs ruled and, until they became **extinct** about 65 million years ago, other animals could not diversify or increase their numbers. The dinosaurs of Gondwana were special and spectacular, though they were related to dinosaurs elsewhere. They included sauropods, ankylosaurs and iguanodonts. When dinosaurs disappeared forever, the way was clear for mammals to expand over the entire world.

Muttaburrasaurus, *an Australian dinosaur.*

The Age of Mammals

After the **extinction** of the dinosaurs, more and more **species** of **mammals** **evolved** in the part of Gondwana that eventually became Australia. They developed weird and wonderful life styles not seen anywhere else on Earth. Without the dinosaurs to hunt them and eat all their food, mammals thrived. They grew gigantic, becoming known as the **megafauna**. There were huge wombats and other **browsers** and cunning **carnivores** armed with lethal weapons, such as teeth and claws. There's more about megafauna on pages 26–37.

Procoptodon goliah *was a huge, prehistoric kangaroo that grew to about 200 kilograms in weight.*

How Do We Know?

How do we know about dinosaurs and other **prehistoric** animal and plant life? Fossil scientists called **palaeontologists** dig up and study fossil teeth and bones of animals **preserved** in layers of **sediment**. If they're really lucky, they find enough pieces of one animal's skeleton to put them together in the shape of the living animal. This helps them identify what animals there were, where and how they lived and what the Earth was like back then. Sometimes, from looking at the bones and teeth, they can reconstruct on a computer what the body of the animal looked like—its shape, its skin and other features. **Fossils** provide us with a picture of our prehistoric ancestors. There's more about fossils on pages 40–43.

A fossil jaw bone of an extinct **Protemnodon** *species (a primitive kangaroo) found in 4 million-year-old sediments in South Australia*

Fly, Run, Hop, Walk or Slither?

Plants can make their own food, but all animals need to move about so they can find food and escape being eaten. Food provides animals with energy for their daily life—to keep warm, to grow, to find more food and to have young.

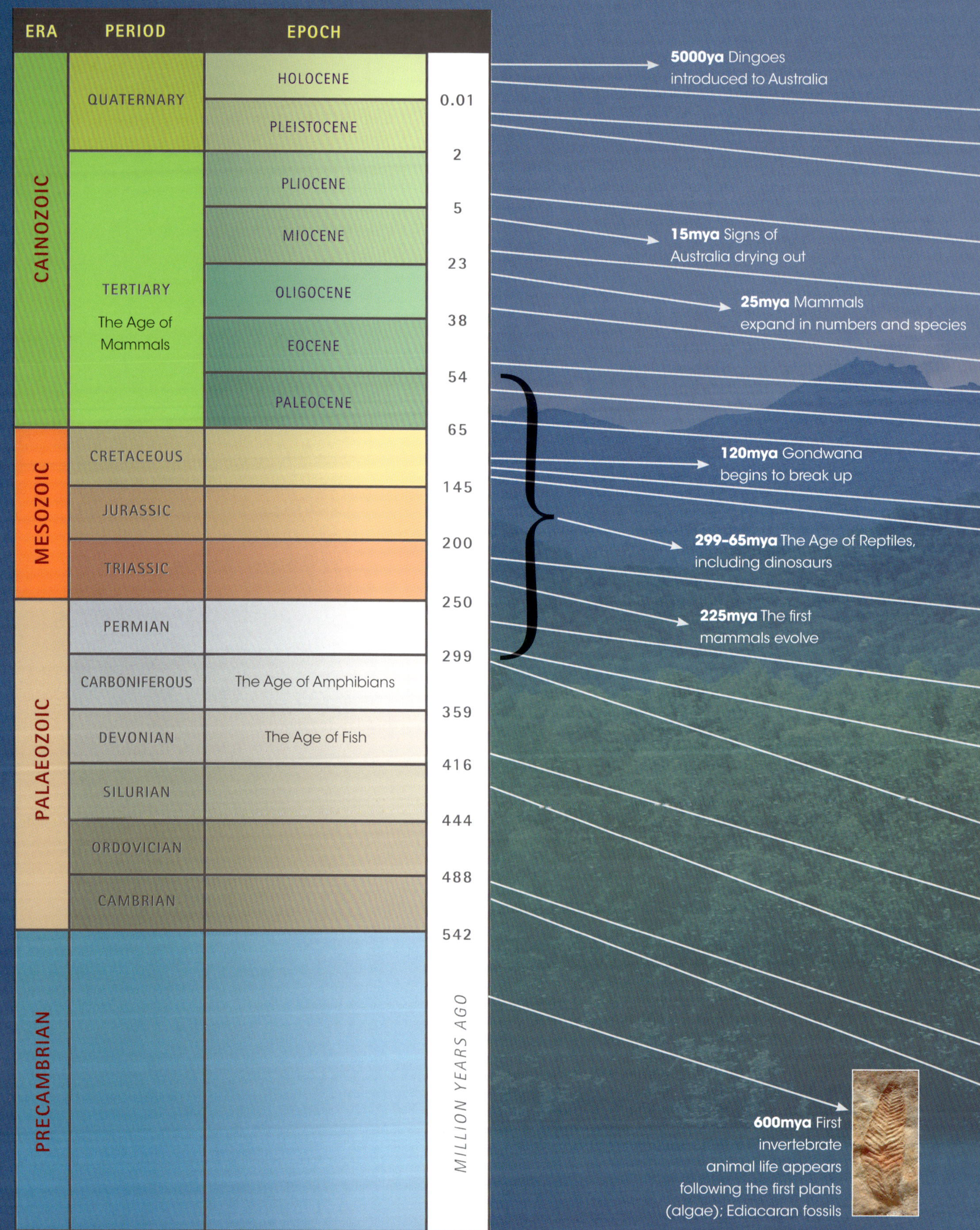
ERA
PERIOD
EPOCH
CAINOZOIC
QUATERNARY
HOLOCENE
PLEISTOCENE
TERTIARY
The Age of Mammals
PLIOCENE
MIOCENE
OLIGOCENE
EOCENE
PALEOCENE
MESOZOIC
CRETACEOUS
JURASSIC
TRIASSIC
PALAEOZOIC
PERMIAN
CARBONIFEROUS
The Age of Amphibians
DEVONIAN
The Age of Fish
SILURIAN
ORDOVICIAN
CAMBRIAN
PRECAMBRIAN
0.01
2
5
23
38
54
65
145
200
250
299
359
416
444
488
542
MILLION YEARS AGO
5000ya Dingoes introduced to Australia
15mya Signs of Australia drying out
25mya Mammals expand in numbers and species
120mya Gondwana begins to break up
299–65mya The Age of Reptiles, including dinosaurs
225mya The first mammals evolve
600mya First invertebrate animal life appears following the first plants (algae); Ediacaran fossils

Time Line

mya = million years ago

Humans: develop agriculture and domesticate animals; invent the wheel; begin using iron; develop writing; develop complex technology and space travel

45 000ya Megafauna extinctions in Australia
60 000ya Humans arrive in Australia

2mya to 100 000ya Large land animals appear. Ice ages come and go.

Climate gets warmer; forests give way to grasslands. Grazing animals and the first humans appear. Megafauna abundant

Australia covered in thick tropical forests

35mya Australia separates from Antarctica

Modern birds evolve

Early mammals expand. They share the land with birds, reptiles, amphibians and invertebrates.

Extinction of dinosaurs. Gondwana broken up except Australia and Antarctica

125mya flowering plants emerge

First feathered birds evolve from dinosaurs

The Age of Dinosaurs begins

Reptiles evolve

Amphibians evolve. Pangea breaks into two lands—Laurasia in the north and Gondwana in the south

Gondwanan plants include moss, ferns and trees such as ginkgoes and cycads

Insects and the first amphibians appear

First animals with shells appear

500mya first fish evolve

Fishes are dominant

Before the Dinosaurs

We can trace **evolution** from the earliest animals that lived in the sea over 600 million years ago. Without them, life as we know it would not exist. Plants and animals have been evolving ever since. Humans have only been around for about 5 million years. Many animals have been here much longer.

***Ediacaran** animals are the first large multi-celled animals known on Earth Their fossils were discovered in the Flinders Ranges, South Australia and date back 600 million years. This is a model of one of them.*

Worms, Starfish and Burrowers

The first living things were in the sea. Some animals, such as flat worms that looked like pieces of ribbon, burrowed into the sea floor, while soft, slug-like animals slithered across it. Crusty starfish and weird crayfish-like creatures scuttled in between and around rocks. These animals had no backbones, and so are called **invertebrates**. From them **evolved** animals with backbones, the **vertebrates**. The first of these were fish, and from the fishes came all other bony animals, including humans.

Bones and Skulls

Vertebrates are the only animals with backbones and a skull. Hard, strong bones make up an internal skeleton. They give the animal its shape and support it while it moves around. The first amphibians had a bony skeleton. A skeleton allows an animal to get big—like the huge dinosaurs. Without their huge skeletons they would not have been able to move around and find food.

Legs and Lungs

The first fish appeared about 500 million years ago. Most remained in the sea and evolved into all the different fish you see today. But others ventured onto land. One group of fish developed legs in place of fins and they swapped **gills** for lungs so they could breathe air. Armed with legs and lungs, they could leave the water and rule the land. Our living Australian lungfish, which can walk on its fins and come out of the water, is a wonderful example of fish to land animal transformation. It is thought to look much like the common ancestors of the land vertebrates.

Taking a Breath

The first land-dwellers were amphibians—as are today's frogs and salamanders (though there are no native salamanders in Australia). The amphibians had developed lungs to breathe air and come out of the water onto the land. However, all amphibians have soft skin and need to lay their eggs in water.

*Many small pieces of information (in the form of fossils) allow **palaeontologists** to build a picture of evolution on Earth. The puzzle pieces here put the evolution of major groups in order.*

Reptiles Rule

Did you know that all dinosaurs were reptiles, but not all reptiles were dinosaurs? About 360 million years ago, one **amphibian** group **evolved** to live entirely on land and became the reptiles. They could lay eggs out of water! They soon adapted to every kind of **habitat**, both on land and in water. There were **herbivores**, **omnivores**, **predators** and **scavengers**. Some even took to the air as **pterodactyls**—flying reptiles. Others returned to the sea and became the **ichthyosaurs**, **mosasaurs** and **plesiosaurs**. Reptiles ruled the land and the seas for 185 million years! Today there are only four groups of reptiles: turtles and tortoises; crocodiles and alligators; snakes and lizards; and *Sphenodon* (tuatara) in New Zealand.

The Age of Dinosaurs

In the last period of the **Mesozoic era**, the **Cretaceous**, from 145 to 65 million years ago, the dinosaurs were the most successful animals walking on the land. Many species grew to gigantic sizes and dominated the environment. The largest dinosaurs, such as sauropods, were **herbivores**. Of the **carnivorous** killer dinosaurs that ran around on their two hind legs, a few, like *Tyrannosaurus rex*, were huge. It was not found on **Gondwana**, though carnivorous *Allosaurus* species were. Today, worldwide, we know of about 500 species of dinosaurs. The Gondwanan dinosaurs are an important part of the dinosaur family.

Huge Teeth, Snarling Killers

When you hear the word dinosaur you probably think of gigantic huge-toothed snarling killers. So it's hard to believe that the first reptiles were small—about the size of a small dog! But from these small beginnings came the huge and amazing reptiles we know as dinosaurs. The word 'dinosaur' comes from the Greek words *deinos*, meaning 'terrible', and *sauros*, meaning 'lizard'. That group of reptiles was named by Richard Owen in 1841. He was a famous British scientist. In fact you could say he invented dinosaurs. The Age of Reptiles, or Dinosaurs, as it is known, was to last about 185 million years and is called the **Mesozoic** era.

Allosaurus *were among the largest carnivorous dinosaurs. This skeleton was found in America—* ***Allosaurus*** *is known in Australia only from a single foot bone.*

The World of Dinosaurs

The life forms present during the Age of Dinosaurs were very different from those of today. There were fewer than half as many species of plants and animals on land. The animals had smaller brains, suggesting that their life was quite slow and simple. The temperature was warmer but not **tropical** as we know it. There were no polar icecaps, but there was ice. Herbivorous dinosaurs ate plants such as cycads and ferns. Today there are more plant species, including rich grasses that animals eat.

Dinosaur Walk

Crocodiles are reptiles that have been around since the earliest reptiles. You can see how, unlike dinosaurs, their legs are at the sides of their body and their belly is close to the ground. Part of the reason dinosaurs were so successful was because of how they walked. All reptiles back then and still today, except for the dinosaurs, had their legs out to the sides of their body, and many drag their belly along the ground. But dinosaurs' legs were underneath their body, holding them upright. They could grow bigger and run faster than other reptiles and so find food more easily.

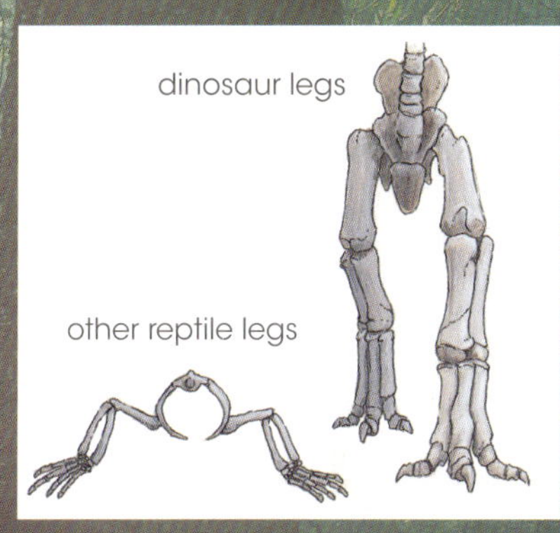

Umoonasaurus *was a* ***plesiosaur*** *that lived in shallow Gondwanan seas. It was only about 2.5 metres long.*

Mesozoic Monsters

The dinosaurs included the biggest animals ever to have walked the Earth. Some were gigantic— up to 135 tonnes—and most of the biggest ones were **vegetarians**. They came in many shapes, with some built like rhinos and others like elephants with long necks and tails. Some ran about on two legs, others on four. But not all of them were giants. There were also chicken-sized dinosaurs. They lived in almost all **habitats** and no other animal group, such as the mammals, could develop because the dinosaurs ate most of the food and took up most of the space.

Living Alongside the Dinosaurs

During the time of the dinosaurs, other animals shared the environment: the ancestors of today's reptiles such as the lizard-like *Sphenodon*, or **tuatara** (say sfen-o-don; two-a-tara) (pictured), whose relatives still survive in New Zealand, lived alongside the dinosaurs. Fish and **amphibians** continued to thrive, and more **species evolved**.

The first **mammals** also lived with the dinosaurs but they remained small (rat to cat size) and were probably **nocturnal** (as most Australian mammals still are) to avoid the dinosaurs, which were **diurnal**.

Meet the Australian Dinosaurs

Fossils of nine different groups of dinosaurs have been discovered in Australia. That's not many, compared to the rest of the world, where more than 500 different kinds of dinosaurs have been found. But Australian/ **Gondwanan** dino-saurs are important because they help to provide a bigger picture of dinosaur **evolution** worldwide. This book covers five groups: sauropods, ankylosaurs, iguanodonts and two groups of theropods.

Stretching and Stones

The shape and worn areas of **sauropod** teeth show they were plant eaters. They ate branches and bark as well as soft ferns and mosses. To reach some of these they would have had to stretch their necks to feed, as a giraffe does. Sauropods carried stones in their stomach to help grind up their food.

Fossil Footprints

To hold their extraordinary weight, sauropod leg and foot bones were arranged to give them a circular 'elephant-like' appearance. Large, fleshy pads on the underside of each foot stopped them getting sore feet! Sometimes the bones of a dinosaur are not found, but we know it existed because we have its footprints. These huge rounded tracks are more than a metre wide and are found at Broome in Western Australia. It is thought that they were made by one of the largest dinosaurs in the world. They also tell us that this sauropod lived on this area of land about 120 million years ago.

Gentle Armoured Leaf Munchers

Despite their fierce appearance, **ankylosaurs** (say an-ki-low-saws) were **herbivores**. As dinosaurs went, they were small to medium-sized **reptiles** about 2-5 metres long. They had a long, wide body, small head and long tail. They had short legs and walked on all four feet. Being close to the ground they would have **browsed** on lower plants such as ferns, cutting them off with their parrot-like beak. Their teeth were small and shaped a bit like a tiny hand with the fingers close together. They made their food into a ball and chewed it just like a cow does today. To escape being eaten, as well as having scales, their skin was covered with extra thick armour plating, called **scutes** (say scoots). Some had a bony club at the end of the tail.

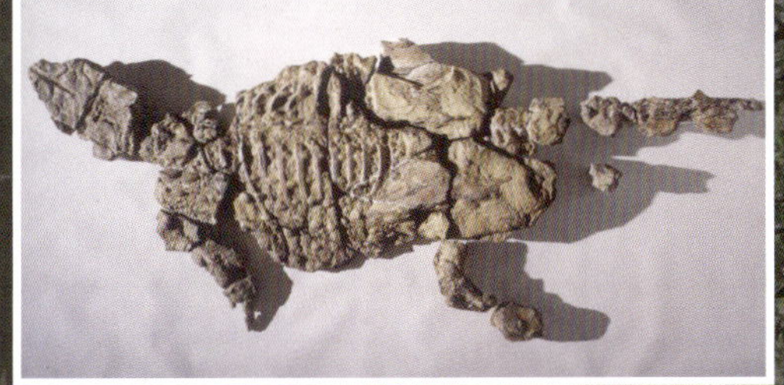

*The most complete ankylosaur skeleton found in Australia is '**Minmi**'. It was discovered in early **Cretaceous** rocks in Queensland in 1964. The fossil contains even the head and the body armour. The animal was 3 metres long. It is one of only two near-complete ankylosaurs ever found in the Southern Hemisphere.*

The Biggest Ever

Sauropods (say saw-ro-pods) came in one size—gigantic! They were the largest of all the dinosaurs ever to have lived, some reaching 40 metres long and weighing 135 tonnes. They had a huge, scaly body, a small head on an extra long neck, and an equally long tail to counterbalance them. They walked on all fours. When you're the biggest dinosaur ever, nothing is going to kill you easily. So sauropods didn't need armour, scutes or spikes to protect themselves, though they did use their long tail as a whip to ward off pesky theropods (see page 17).

*One sauropod that lived in Australia during the **Cretaceous** period was **Austrosaurus**. It would have been one of the largest land animals ever to have lived.*

Bird-Footed Dinosaurs

Iguanodonts (say igg-wan-o-donts) are part of the large group of dinosaurs called **ornithopods** (say orn-ith-o-pods), which means 'bird feet'. They had three forward-pointing toes on each hind foot, like birds. They existed for almost the entire time of the dinosaurs. (Some other dinosaurs that **evolved** in the early part of the Triassic period died out and were replaced by more modern ones during the **Jurassic** and **Cretaceous** periods.) They ranged in size from 1 metre tall and 2 metres long up to 7 metres tall and 20 metres long. They walked upright on their powerful hind limbs. Their front limbs were also sometimes strong enough to use for walking. Iguanodonts inhabited the entire forested world of the time.

Fast Feet versus Flesh Rippers

In a world dominated by theropods (see page 17), you would think that **iguanodonts**, being small dinosaurs, would need lots of armour plate and spikes to protect them. But they had neither. They did have a claw more than 15 centimetres long on each thumb, which would have been useful in combat. But mostly they would run on their heavy hind legs to escape from **predators**, much like herds of deer run from a lion or cheetah. These methods of protection obviously worked well, because they became one of the largest and longest lived families of any dinosaur. Iguanodonts probably lived in herds.

A Speedy Aussie

Muttaburrasaurus is the most complete dinosaur skeleton ever discovered in Australia. It was an iguanodont-type dinosaur, named after the station of Muttaburra in Queensland, where it was discovered, and *sauros* for lizard. Its spectacular reconstructed skeleton shows that it walked on all fours. Being an iguanodont it could also have walked and run on its extremely strong, powerful back legs. It would have been an amazing sight. At 10 metres long and 5 metres high, it was a medium-sized iguanodont.

Muttaburrasaurus had a bony bump on its snout near to where its nostrils were. Could this be some sort of structure for making sound to communicate with other iguanodonts? We will never know.

A Famous Dinosaur

Iguanodonts are among the most famous of all the dinosaurs. An iguanodont was the very first dinosaur ever to be discovered, and this was in England. Gideon Mantell, the geologist who discovered it in 1822, described it as a lizard of 'enormous magnitude'. He named it *Iguanodon* because he thought the teeth resembled those of an iguana lizard. Iguanodonts had a rounded parrot-like beak, but without the point. This allowed them to select the plant leaves they wanted to eat—they did not just grab at plants, break off bits and gulp. Having specialised teeth in many rows, and cheek pouches, iguanodonts chewed their food before swallowing.

Meat-Ripping Killers

Theropods were cunning, deadly, meat-ripping killers. *Tyrannosaurus rex* was one of them. They had strong jaws and dagger-like, slightly curved teeth with jagged front edges. With these they could cut through huge chunks of flesh, which they then swallowed whole. Their fearsome toothy smile would have been enough to scare most unsuspecting dinosaurs, no matter what their size. As most dinosaurs were **herbivores**, theropods had plenty to eat. Theropods survived for more than 160 million years and include some of the oldest of any dinosaurs. **Fossils** of theropods date back about 230 million years.

Small Aussie Theropod

Allosaurus was one type of theropod. Fossil *Allosaurus* found in Victoria were small—only about 5 metres long and 2 metres high. Elsewhere in the world they were up to 12 metres long. In other parts of the world, *Allosaurus* became **extinct** in the Jurassic period (about 145 million years ago) but the Australian *Allosaurus* was a 'living fossil' that survived into the **Cretaceous** period.

Running Hunters

Many four-legged vegetarian dinosaurs were like medieval knights. They had armour plating, spikes, whip-lashing tails, ball-like clumps on the end of their tail and they were huge. But even with so many ways of protecting themselves the **theropods** could still get them. The strong, slender theropods were the only dinosaurs with hollow bones. This made them lighter, so they could run fast on their hind legs. They used speed, size, cunning, claws and teeth to catch their prey. Their hands were armed with deadly curved claws with which they could grasp and hold their prey.

Terrible Lizards Of The Sea

Australia also had terrifying reptiles during the Age of Dinosaurs that were not dinosaurs. These were the **mosasaurs**, **plesiosaurs** and **ichthyosaurs**. They once lived on land, but returned to live in the shallow seas both around the coast and inland, just as millions of years later various groups of land **mammals** did the same, becoming dolphins, whales and seals. Although they adapted to live in a watery world, they remained air-breathers and needed to surface to breathe.

*This model of an **Elasmosaurus** skull shows what the head of a plesiosaur may have looked like. The ferocious curved teeth may have been used to catch fish which it would swallow whole. It probably swallowed stones to help grind up the food in its stomach. Fossils of the animal were found in the Andamooka opal fields in South Australia, which back in the early Cretaceous period were part of a huge inland sea.*

*The **Pliosaurus** was a short-necked plesiosaur. It would take fish or other animals from the sea floor and swallow them whole.*

*The **Elasmosaurus** was a long-necked plesiosaur . Its body and neck was up to 10 metres long, while its head was less than 50 centimetres long. It ate shellfish that it took from the sea floor.*

Plesiosaurs

Plesiosaurs were also related to lizards and snakes, and had a sea-snake-like appearance. Some of these marine **reptiles** were small, such as *Umoonasaurus*. Others were gigantic, bigger than the largest dinosaurs on the land at the time. With a mouth full of sharp teeth some, such as *Kronosaurus*, found in Queensland, were the meanest looking **carnivores** ever to have lived. Some plesiosaurs had long necks, while others had shorter necks.

*This fossil **mosasaur** head came from Canada. Mosasaurs were predators with large heads and big teeth.*

Mosasaurs

Mosasaurs were reptiles, closely related to monitor lizards or goannas. They may have also been the distant ancestor of snakes. They were equipped with ferocious teeth and swam using four flippers and swaying their tail from side to side, much as a crocodile does today. They would have lived in central Queensland inland seas of the **Mesozoic** period and eaten plesiosaurs.

Ichthyosaurs—'Fish-reptiles'

Ichthyosaurs were reptiles, but their bodies were fish-like. They were adapted to a life in the sea. Many looked like a cross between a dolphin and a shark but scientists believe they were more closely related to lizards and snakes.

From Scales to Feathers and Fur

From **reptiles evolved** the other animals you can see around you today. Mammals such as kangaroos and wombats started out as tiny animals that lost their scales and gained fur. Birds, too, came from one of the main groups of dino-saur reptiles—their scales changed into feathers. If you look at a bird you can see that they still have scales on their legs and feet.

Early Mammals

Steropodon (say ster-opo-don) was an early ***monotreme****. But unlike the modern ones—platypus and echidna—Steropodon had powerful jaws and teeth. It probably fed in the water on crustaceans and small fish.*

Mammals did not **evolve** from dinosaurs but from an early type of prehistoric reptile. These primitive mammals were small, mouse to cat-sized animals that lived alongside the dinosaurs. To remain safe, they were probably **nocturnal** and tried to avoid dinosaurs. Just as an elephant cannot see a mouse running around its feet, nor could dinosaurs usually see the tiny furry mammals beneath them. It must have been awfully scary for a tiny fur-ball to get from one place to another when a herd of sauropods came plodding along.

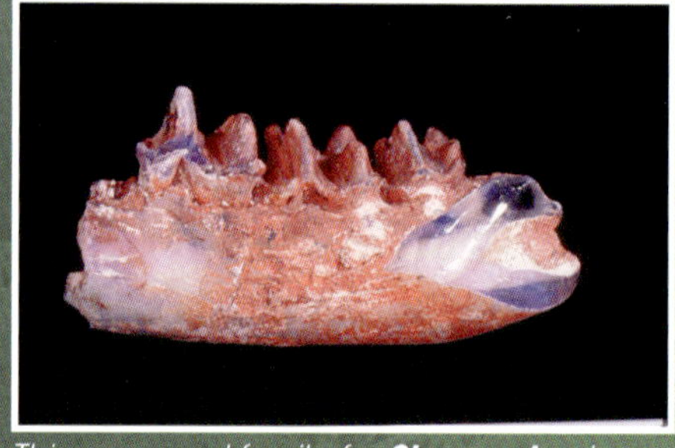

This pure opal fossil of a ***Steropodon*** *jaw with teeth was found at Lightning Ridge in New South Wales. The name Steropodon means 'lightning tooth'.*

Kollikodon

Kollikodon (say koll-iek-o-don) is thought to be one of the most primitive **mammals** ever to have been found. It was named after the shape of its teeth. The Greek word *killokos* means 'bun-like', and odous is Greek for 'tooth'. *Kollikodon* had weird teeth that look like hot cross buns! The shape of the teeth suggests that it ate a range of foods, including hard-shelled animals such as shellfish. This also tells us that it hunted in water so it was a swimmer. The only place **fossils** of this mammal have ever been found in the entire world is at Lightning Ridge in New South Wales. That makes it a special Australian treasure.

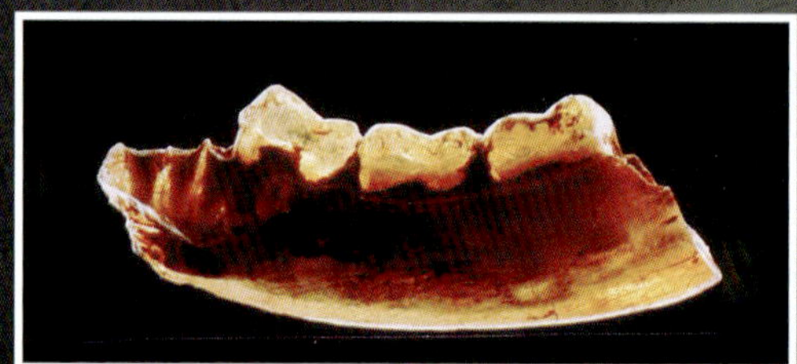

This ***Kollikodon*** *jaw and teeth have become opalised. The jaws, with teeth, of several different types of small* ***prehistoric*** *mammals have been found in Australia. Teeth are treasure to palaeontologists who study mammals as they reveal a great deal about the animal.*

Dino-birds

What does the fierce flesh-ripping Australian theropod ***Allosaurus*** have in common with the Emu? Plenty, as birds are feathered descendants of dinosaurs! It is hard to imagine that theropods—**carnivores** and fiercest of all the dinosaurs—were the distant cousins of today's birds. It's amazing to think that such a tough, scaly **predator** could evolve into a delicate feathered bird—but it did! In Australia, feathers have been found in dinosaur-aged rocks—perhaps from a bird, or a dinosaur, or a dino-bird. Scientists are still looking for clues about Australia's first flying birds. They believe dino-birds must have existed on **Gondwana**. Early birds that lived with the dinosaurs have been found in Australia.

Archaeopteryx*, the first bird, lived 150 million years ago. This fossil was discovered in Germany.*

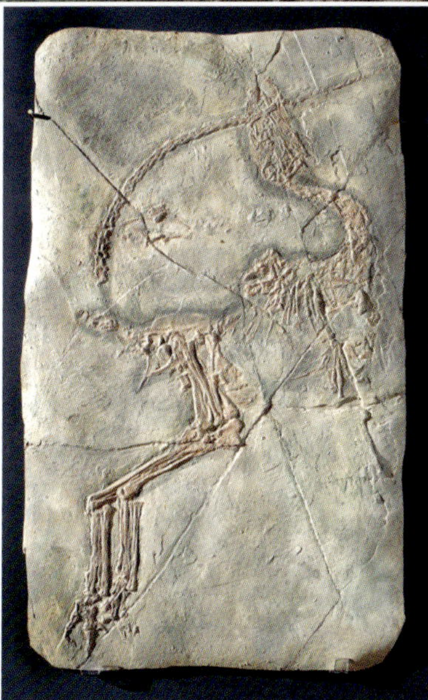

*For many years, scientists couldn't find any clues for the transformation from scales to feathers—**fossils** showing dinosaurs with feathers. But in 1996 amazing feathered fossils were found in China. They provide strong evidence that modern birds did indeed come from one group of ancient dinosaurs. This fossil shows a **Sinosauropteryx**, a feathered dinosaur that lived in China.*

Archaeopteryx the Dino-bird

Archaeopteryx (say ark-key-op-ter-ix) was neither a bird nor a dinosaur—it was a dino-bird. It provides proof of **evolution**. It had well-developed wings and a bird-like skull, together with the teeth and long tail typical of theropod dinosaurs. *Archaeopteryx* lived during the late Jurassic time, around 159–144 million years ago. It was bigger than a rosella, but smaller than a chicken. Following *Archaeopteryx*, true birds soon evolved. They developed many different sizes and shapes and adapted to many **habitats**.

After the Dinosaurs

Australia, with the ancient Gondwanan animals and plants, separates from Antarctica.

About 65 million years ago the dinosaurs became **extinct**. **Gondwana** had almost split apart. Australia was the last to separate, making the break from Antarctica about 35 million years ago. Australia then slid northwards over the surface of the planet. From this time forward, Australia was isolated from all other continents. Unique plants and animals, such as the first kangaroos and koalas, began to **evolve** from their Gondwanan ancestors. This happened over millions of years.

New Land, New Animals

During the Miocene epoch, about 23–5 million years ago, early relatives of many of today's animals evolved, including possums, kangaroos, koalas, bats, crocodiles, snakes, lizards, frogs and many kinds of bird. But in addition to these familiar animals there were some less well-known ones, such as marsupial lions, flesh-eating kangaroos, thunder birds and horned turtles.

***Marsupials** evolved about 120 million years ago. Today, Australia has some 300 species of marsupials, including four species of Quoll, one of which is pictured here.*

A Leafy Land

The new land of Australia was covered in the primitive mosses, ferns and giant forest trees from Gondwana. But just as the new animals were evolving, so were the plants. From about 15 million years ago, in the Miocene, the Australian land mass crumpled up against the South-East Asian land mass. Australia was now covered in thick warm **tropical** rainforest. Plants and vines grew on the trunks of the huge trees and the forest floor was a green carpet of many smaller leafy plants. Thick green forests spread out across the land, providing the perfect **habitat** for an amazing variety of animal life.

Now There are Five

Earlier we discovered that all **vertebrate** animals **evolved** from life in the sea. First there were **invertebrates**. Then came the fish, from which came the **amphibians**, followed by the **reptiles**. Then the path to modern vertebrates stopped for millions of years until the **extinction** of the dinosaurs allowed other vertebrate animals to evolve. Only then could the last two major vertebrate classes—birds and **mammals**—evolve into the **dominant** groups they are today. Members of all five groups—fish, amphibians, reptiles, birds and mammals—continue to share the planet. During this 'age of mammals' from 65 million years to the present, many hundreds of thousands of unique animals inhabited the sea, land and air.

Mammals Rule

Mammals could only begin to expand in their **species** and numbers when the dinosaurs became extinct. The first mammals developed an outer covering of hair, wool or fur to keep warm. They laid eggs, just like all of the other animal groups up until this time. They were to remain here in Australia as Platypus and echidnas. But with the mammals' expansion came new ways to have offspring. **Marsupial** mammals **evolved** to care for their tiny offspring in a pouch.

***Emus** are giant, very primitive flightless birds endemic to Australia. They, and their relatives the Ostrich and Cassowary, are probably the closest living relatives of dinosaurs.*

Feathers Replace Scales

The dinosaurs became **extinct** 65 million years ago. But birds are the living descendants of one group of dinosaurs, the theropods. Feathers are made up of the same material as **scutes**, the thick scales on all reptiles. Birds have scales on their feet and legs. All birds could fly once and most still do. But some, such as the ancient birds that came from Gondwana, like Emu, Cassowary, Ostrich, Moa, Kiwi and Rhea adapted for walking. They became big and heavy and lost the ability to fly.

The Age of Mammals

With the **extinction** of the dinosaurs, a new and exciting age unfolded. **Mammals evolved** to occupy all **habitats** in the world, from the cold Antarctic to the rainforests and hot deserts. Mammals expanded to fill the new land of Australia, with its developing variety of habitats. First came the **monotremes**—for example platypus and, much later, echid-na—then the **marsupials** and **placentals**.

Mammals and birds—unlike reptiles (including dinosaurs), fish and **amphibians**—could generate their own heat. A covering of hair or feathers helped to keep the heat in and their body temperature constant. Not needing the sun to be active, they could live in more types of habitats.

Inefficient Egg Layers

All the most primitive land **vertebrates** laid eggs. The birds, most **reptiles** and the first tiny waddling monotremes laid eggs. But egg-laying is an inefficient and unreliable way to have offspring. Many eggs were eaten by other animals. Others died because the parents could not keep them warm enough. Mammals evolved new, more efficient ways of bearing young.

*An **Echidna** egg is smaller than a five-cent piece!*

*A **Diamond Python** laying eggs.*

***Echidnas** are primitive egg-laying mammals.*

Mammals Around the World

In Australia 55 million years ago there were both placental and marsupial mammals, but the marsupials won the race and survived to the present. Bats are the only placental mammals to have survived from that time here, though they have since been joined by others, for example dingoes, foxes, cats and rats. In South America marsupials also ruled among mammals but in the Northern Hemisphere and in Africa placental mammals dominated.

Bats are placental mammals. This mother is with its baby in a nursery roost in a cave.

Live Births—Marsupials versus Placentals

Some mammals **evolved** a new way to develop and care for their eggs. They keep not only the egg, but the **embryo**, inside their body until the baby develops further. Marsupial females give birth to a tiny, underdeveloped baby that climbs up into a warm, furry pouch. Here it is protected and feeds on milk from a teat while it continues to develop. Placental females went a step further. They keep the baby inside their body until it is fully developed. When the young are born they also suck milk from a teat, but not in a pouch.

Kangaroos are marsupials whose young develop in a pouch

Diprotodons–Gentle Munchers and Grazers

This picture shows a **diprotodon** leg bone next to that of a modern-day wombat.

Just imagine an animal the size of a car, or bigger, walking slowly towards you! One would have scared you, let alone a herd of them. They were the biggest marsupials anywhere in the world. But you would be amazed not only by their huge size, but also by their gentle nature. **Diprotodon fossils** have been found over a wide area, from Riversleigh in Queensland to caves at Naracoorte in South Australia and Wellington in New South Wales. Diprotodon probably lived in herds on lowland areas where open forest meets grassland.

The Largest Marsupial Ever

Diprotodon optatum (say di-proto-don op-tat-umm) was a giant weighing about 2000 kilograms, about the same as a rhinoceros. This animal was a beast! But for all its huge size it had a small brain. It is thought to have had a 'wombat-type' nose and shaggy hair. Like its relative the wombat, diprotodon probably had a backwards-facing pouch—wombats dig; the pouch opening facing backwards stops dirt getting into the nursery. Diprotodons were probably too big to dig burrows. Their huge size would have protected them from most **predators**.

***Diptrotodon** skull found at Redbanks Reserve in South Australia.*

Huge Munching Teeth

Diprotodonts included **browsing vegetarians** such as wombats, koalas, kangaroos and possums, as well as large predatory marsupial lions. These different animals do not really look much alike. But if you could open their mouths, with great care, you would be able to see the family resemblance in their teeth! They all have two bottom front teeth. The word diprotodon comes from the Greek words *di* (two), *proto* (front) and *don* (tooth). Diprotodons used their two pairs of huge front teeth, one at the top and one at the bottom, to cut off their plant food. Their powerful molars (back teeth) would grind it up. Because of their huge size, they would have needed to eat a lot.

***Diprotodons** had giant teeth for grinding vegetation.*

A Marsupial with a Trunk?

Palorchestes azael (say pal-or-kes-tees) was a weird relative of diprotodon that also lived in **Pleistocene** times. This giant **marsupial** was about the size of a donkey, but looked more like a tapir as it had a short trunk. It also probably had a long, giraffe-like tongue that it curled around bunches of leaves to bite off a decent mouthful at a time. We do not know whether they ate leaves from trees or from ground plants. But they had huge 6 centimetre-long razor-sharp claws and powerful forearms. Maybe they dug for tree roots, or ripped open termite mounds to get at the insects. They were too big to climb trees.

The Age of Megafauna

Many different **species** of **mammals** lived side by side. They became very successful and in the period 25–2 million years ago many developed into giant animals that we call **megafauna**. They grew biggest in the Pleistocene, between 2 million and 50 000 years ago. They were big in size, big in numbers and big in diversity. Australia's megafaunal mam-mals were all marsupials, but there were also mega-**reptiles** and mega-birds.

Giant Wombats

The first Aborigines arrived in Australia across a land bridge from Asia around 60 000 years ago. They would have certainly come into contact with the megafauna and especially the huge **diprotodons**. Diprotodons are related to our modern-day wombats.

Phascolonus gigas *(say fas-co-lo-nus gig-as) was a giant Pleistocene wombat from the diprotodon group that stood about 1 metre high, was over 1.5 metres long and weighed about 200 kilograms. Like today's wombats, it probably had a backwards-facing pouch and short hair covering its body. It had huge claws and, being a close relative of wombats, probably did dig burrows. Just imagine the size of its burrows!*

Here a modern-day wombat is shown beside ***Phascolonus gigas****, giving an idea of the size comparison.*

The Koala Clan

You are walking through the trees with the sun making wonderful patterns on the ground all around, when you notice there is a big shady patch up ahead. You look up into the trees and see a giant fur ball asleep. It is so big you wonder how the branches can hold its weight and not send the monster crashing down on top of you! The koala family first **evolved** at least 25 million years ago. Just like their cousins the wombats, koalas have a backwards-facing pouch. So far at least 12 fossil **species** are known, including some that were twice the size. Sadly, all have become **extinct** except for the one **species** that survives today.

Part of the skull of Koala ancestor ***Nimiokoala****, found at Riversleigh in Queensland.*

Giant Koala

Some fossil bones of Koala ancestors, such as *Phascolarctos* and *Nimiokoala*, that have been unearthed show that it was twice the size of the Koala you see in the trees today. Males were larger than females, growing to 1.6 metres long and 27 kilograms; females weighed about 16 kilograms. These mega-koalas lived more than 40 000 years ago. They too, just like modern Koalas, did little more than eat and sleep. Being such huge animals, they would need to carefully choose the trees they lived in to avoid breaking them!

Life in the Slow Lane

All koalas came from a ground-dwelling ancestor. Koalas adapted to life in the trees to avoid competition for food. There they stayed, where predators could not easily catch them. But sometimes they do come down to the ground to get from tree to tree or to a new area. No-one could say that today's Koalas do not looked relaxed. Even a sloth in the Amazon rainforest looks more energetic than a Koala. Superbly adapted to live way up in gum trees, their behinds firmly planted in the forks of branches, they can safely chew leaves and nap all day and watch the world go slowly by.

The Kangaroo Clan

Apart from the Koala, kangaroos are the most famous Australian animals. Today there are more than 52 different kinds of kangaroos, and they come in all shapes and sizes. But the **extinct** kangaroos were the most weird and won-derful of all, and some were huge! Kangaroos once inhabited **tropical** forests and would have had a much tastier vari-ety of plants to dine on compared to the grass modern-day kangaroos eat.

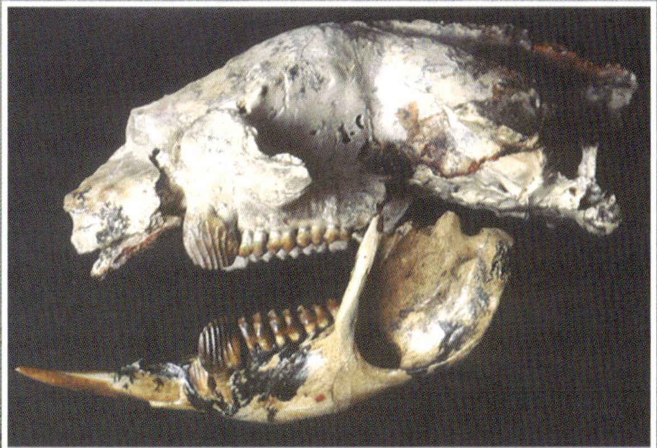

Killer Carniroo

Imagine that you spotted a kangaroo chewing on the remains of a bird. Could this really be true? Although most **prehistoric** kangaroos were plant-eaters, some were **carnivores** with specialised teeth to prove it. They hunted and killed animals. Pictured is the skull of a giant rat-kangaroo-like animal called ***Ekaltadeta***. It shows that this powerful, robust killer probably took large prey. It could grip prey with its front arms and huge claws and use its powerful jaws and huge teeth to bite and kill.

The Largest Roo

Apart from being the largest kangaroo ever, ***Procoptodon goliah*** (say pro-cop-toe-don goh-lia) was strange. It had a face that looked as if it had hopped full speed into a very large tree. It had a pushed-in stubby nose, forward-facing eyes and large, powerful jaws. On its hind foot was single long toe with a strong, hoof-like claw. Its hands had two extra-long fingers with large claws. Maybe it used these as tools to claw off pieces of bark or reach up for branches full of sweet leaves. Its fossil bones have been found at many sites around Australia, such as Naracoorte in South Australia and the Darling Downs in Queensland.

Lean, Mean Killing Machines

During the late **Pleistocene**, two of the top **carnivores** were marsupials, distant relatives to wombats! One of these was the marsupial lion. It was even more powerful and ferocious than any modern-day lion or other big cat. Amazing as it may sound, it **evolved** from plant eaters, something few predators in the world have done. Grazing animals walked under low-lying branches at their peril, in case one dropped on them from above. The other was the marsupial tiger, or thylacine, which was more like a dog or tiger in appearance and was a ground hunter.

Top Lion

Thylacoleo carnifex was the biggest marsupial carnivore ever to live in Australia—about 1.5 metres in length and 98 kilograms in weight. About the size of a lioness but more heavily built, it was the top **predator** and would have easily killed a young **diprotodon** twice its own weight! Almost complete *Thylacaleo* fossil skeletons have been unearthed in some parts of Australia. Fossil bones of large animals with the tell-tale tooth marks of *Thylacoleo* have also been found. Like all marsupials, the female would have developed the young in her pouch.

Killer Claws and Teeth

Being a killer, ***Thylacoleo*** was armed with amazing weapons on its front feet. Each of its thumbs had a lethal 'switch blade', a large retractable claw it could flick out and grip and rip with when killing prey. Their teeth were superbly adapted for killing and chopping up prey They had two unusual enlarged front teeth that were long and strong for stabbing and two unique giant slicing teeth one above the other on each side. With hugely powerful jaws these teeth would have cut through flesh and bones with ease like bolt cutters.

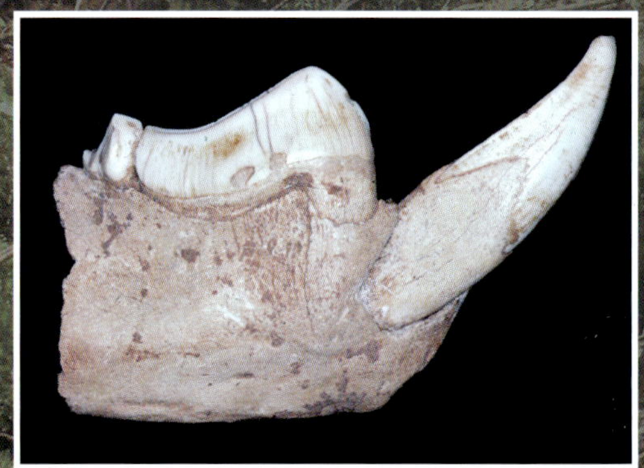

Death by Surprise

For a long time scientists couldn't agree on how **Thylacoleo** hunted for food. They now believe that it would drop down out of a tree onto an unsuspecting animal, sink its thumb claws into it and hold on tight. With its massive mouth and teeth it would deliver the killer bite.

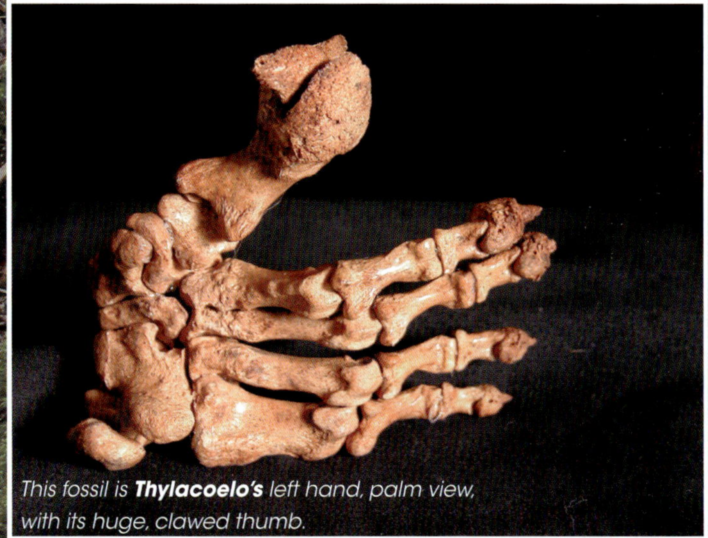

*This fossil is **Thylacoelo's** left hand, palm view, with its huge, clawed thumb.*

A Tiger Like No Other

This may look a bit like a tiger with those stripes but that is as far as it goes. Thylacines (say thy-la-seen) were amazing, mean killing machines. No animal was safe when they were hungry. No wonder koalas took to the trees! They were named from the Greek words *thylakos* meaning 'pouched', and *kynos* meaning 'dog'. Since the late Oligocene, about 25 million years ago, at least eight **species** of thylacine have roamed Australia. Not all lived at the same time, and they ranged from the size of a rat to that of a dog. Thylacines were marsupials unique to Australia. The whole family became **extinct** in the 1930s when the last species of thylacine was exterminated by hunters. It is a sad ending for a family that lived here for millions of years. Tasmania was the last surviving refuge of the thylacine, so they have been commonly called Tasmanian Tigers.

Dried carcasses of thylacines have been found in some Australian caves.

Wolf, Tiger, Dog?

The **thylacine** has also been given the names wolf, for the way it stood, tiger, because it had stripes on its back, and dog because it had bones and a skull that were similar to the dog family. But the thylacine was not anything like a wolf or a tiger. Being a **predator** it was strongly built. Its head and body length was about 1.5 metres and it weighed about 35 kilograms. Unlike dogs (including wolves) and cats (including tigers), which both have rounded rears, the thylacine had a sloping rear that merged with the tail. In **placental mammals** the skeleton shape allows the female to carry a big baby inside her body. **Marsupials**, which include thylacines, only carry a tiny baby inside their body, and the skeleton allows for the baby to grow in a pouch.

Dinosaur-Sized Birds

It's hard to imagine a bird as big as some dinosaurs at 3 metres tall and weighing 500 kilograms! But Australia had such birds. Mihirungs (say mihi-rungs) were a group of huge, flightless birds found only in Australia. There were at least eight **species**. Mihirungs once lived in many areas of Australia—their **fossils** have been found in most States. One fossil that may belong to this group is about 55 million years old, but mihirungs are not certainly known to have existed until 25 million years ago. By then they were already huge, flightless birds. Fossil deposits show that often two species lived together. The last species finally became **extinct** about 45 000 years ago.

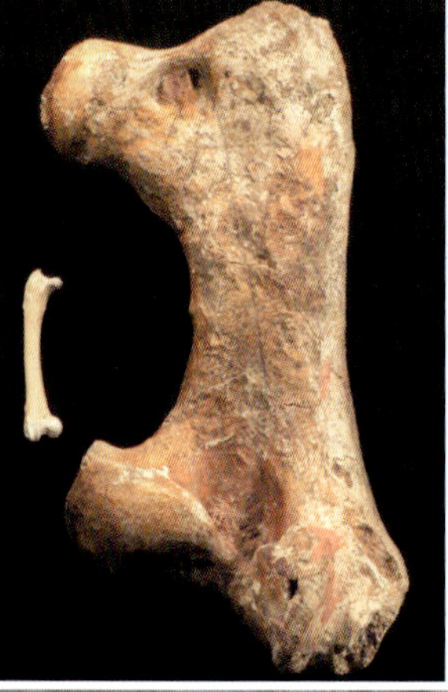

__Mihirungs__ had extremely strong thick leg bones to carry their weight. They could run only at about 15 kilometres per hour compared to emus, which run at about 50 kilometres per hour. Emus hold their wings out when they run, but the wings of the mihirungs were so small you would not have seen them. The picture shows the leg bone of a mihirung next to one of a chicken.

Demon Ducks

The name **mihirung** comes from an Aboriginal legend that tells about 'giant emus' that once lived on the land. They also have nicknames, for example 'thunder birds'. They were so big that running flocks must have sounded like thunder! They have also been called 'demon ducks' because they were more closely related to the duck family than any other birds. They would have been the meanest looking ducks ever!

The Ugly Duckling

Ever since the first mihirung fossil bones were found, it has been a mystery what these birds were related to. Because they were big and could not fly, and because they lived here in Australia, scientists thought they were related to Emus and Cassowaries. Mihirungs may have looked like oversized Emus from afar, but up close you would immediately notice the huge head and beak—Emus and Cassowaries have much smaller heads. Now scientists know that mihirungs are related to ducks, and especially to the **Magpie Goose** (pictured). The clues lie in the details of recently found fossil skulls.

No Budgie seed for this Bird!

Mihirungs had an impressive bill—but did it kill? Because of their size and strength some scientists once thought mihirungs were **carnivores**. Now they know that these weird 'ducks' ate plants. But how do they know this? Plant eaters have gizzard stones in their stomach to grind up and help them digest plant fibre. Mihirungs had gizzards—polished gizzard stones have been found with the fossil bird bones. Their huge, strong beaks would have allowed them to clip off pieces of tough plants—they could have eaten cycad leaves and fruit. Mihirungs also had stout, hoofed feet—they were slow, not agile, and lacked the claws seen in all predators. The skull of the biggest type is nearly the largest bird skull ever found, at 520 millimetres long and 260 millimetres deep, but only about 65 millimetres wide.

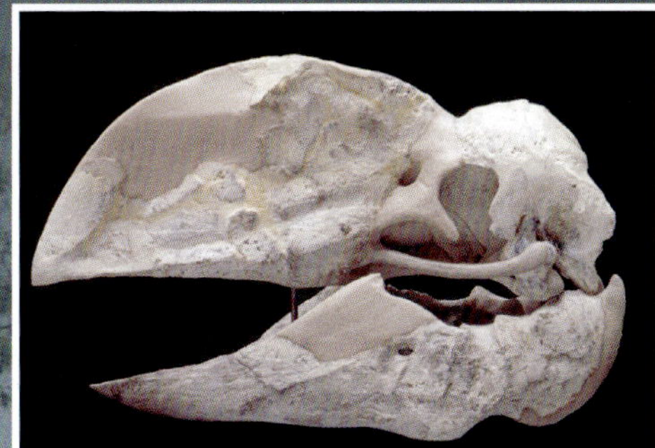

You can see how big the mihirung was when you put its skull next to that of an Emu

*At about 300 kilograms, the **Elephant Bird** of Madagascar was thought to be the heaviest of the big birds.*

Other Big Birds

The **extinct** giant moa from New Zealand, which reached a height of about 2.5 metres, was always thought to be the biggest bird ever to have lived. But some mihirungs were bigger and had a much larger head. The different mihirungs were about 2-3 metres in height and ranged in weight from about 70 kilograms (similar to a Cassowary) to 500 kilograms—possibly the largest bird ever to have lived.

Biggest Bird Ever!

Dromornis stirtoni, one of the mihirungs, is the largest bird ever discovered. Many **fossils** ranging in age from the late Miocene to the Early Pliocene (8 to 4 million years old) have been found in the Northern Territory. With its broad back over 2 metres above the ground and its gigantic half-metre long head towering nearly 3 metres above the ground, and weighing more than 500 kilograms, this mihirung more than matched the moa and the elephant bird.

Squeezers, Swallowers and Rippers

As many of Australia's plant-eating **prehistoric** beasts slowly **evolved** to mega-size over millions of years, the predators either had to do the same or become **extinct**. So, just as the dinosaurs had done before them, other reptiles came to hold the title of reptile rulers. They lived in the **Pleistocene** and grew enormous. Giant predatory lizards, snakes and crocodiles were able to hunt and kill huge prey.

Huge Teeth and Claws

Megalania was a top predator. It would have ambushed diprotodons, attacking and eating them for dinner. *Megalania* teeth were dinosaur-like—all the same size, sharp and curved backwards in huge, strong jaws. As well as these perfect biting and ripping weapons, they had claws more than 6 centimetres long that they could sink into prey. Like the Komodo Dragon today, *Megalania* ate probably anything it could catch and kill, including **mammals**, snakes, other reptiles and birds. *Megalania* **fossils** have been found at many sites in inland Australia. They include a partial skeleton that has provided scientists with a good idea of their size and shape.

*This reconstruction was based on **Megalania** bones found in Queensland and a Komodo Dragon skeleton.*

Ancient Giant Butcher

Megalania (say mega-lane-ia) was the largest lizard on the planet since the dinosaurs. It lived 1 600 000–40 000 years ago during the **Pleistocene** time. Like modern goannas, they probably inhabited open forests, woodlands and grasslands. *Megalania* means 'ancient giant butcher' which is a really good name to describe this monstrous goanna. Of all land reptiles, only some crocodiles and dinosaurs were bigger. It grew to about 6 metres long and weighed up to 600 kilograms—as much as a cow! The largest lizard today, the Komodo Dragon or Ora of Komodo Island in Indonesia, reaches about 3 metres in length and 166 kilograms.

A Smiling Crocodile?

If you look at a crocodile it often looks as if it is smiling. ***Pallimnarchus*** (say pall-um-nark-us) was huge. Not even the biggest of animal was safe from ending up in this croc's stomach! Having a full belly would have given it lots to smile about! *Pallimnarchus* did not look much like modern crocodiles. It had a broad, flat snout, and eyes that were more on the top of its head rather than to the sides. This would have made it good at ambushing **predators** from under the water.

This illustration shows how scientists reconstruct prehistoric animals, starting by drawing the bones, then the muscles, then the skin.

Underwater Stalker

Pallimnarchus reached about 10 metres long and would have weighed close to 2 tonnes, with jaws and teeth to match. *Pallimnarchus* was a powerful killer. It would have attacked and grabbed its prey, holding it with powerful jaws and sharp stabbing teeth. Once the prey was dead, possibly drowned, this giant crocodile would rip off chunks of flesh and swallow them whole. It lived in the fresh waterways of the warmer parts of Australia, where it could stalk prey such as giant kangaroos or a **diprotodon** grazing around the water's edge.

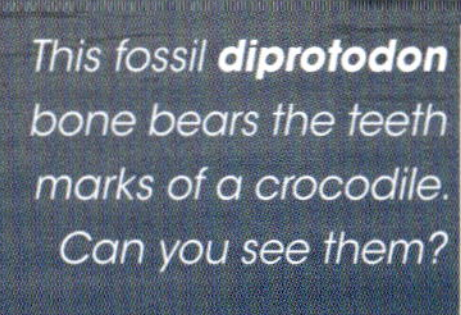

*This fossil **diprotodon** bone bears the teeth marks of a crocodile. Can you see them?*

*You can see the large sockets in the **Pallimnarchus** jawbone where the teeth fit. The tooth is next to the coin.*

Killer Coilers and Weaponed Turtles

Some of the mega-**reptiles** that evolved here in Australia devised wonderful methods of protection. Giant snakes could lie along branches using camouflage as a means of protection against larger **predators** such as lizards or crocodiles. *Ninjemys* turtles protected themselves with armour.

A Prehistoric Hero

Ninjemys lived during the late Pleistocene from about 1 million to about 10 000 years ago. It was one of a number of **species** of horned turtles that lived in Australia from about 100 million years ago. They came from an ancient **Gondwanan** turtle. *Ninjemys* was named from the cartoon TV show 'Ninja Turtles', whose stars were heroic armed turtles. Turtles are a very successful group of reptiles. They evolved during the time of the dinosaurs and have outlived the dinosaurs by 65 million years. They are true survivors.

An Armoured Turtle

Ninjemys oweni (say ninj-emees), like all turtles, was a herbivore. It had bull-sized horns, a bony club on its tail and thick, bony plates covering its legs. Its shell and skeleton would have been very strong to protect it against predators such as *Thylacoleo*, *Megalania* and *Pallimnarchus*. *Ninjemys* measured 2 metres long, more than twice the size of the Galapagos Turtle, which is the largest living turtle. But like the Galapagos Turtle, *Ninjemys* was land based. It had short legs and elephant-like feet, instead of the flippers of sea turtles.

A Giant Python

Today's Olive Python is one of Australia's largest snakes, reaching about 6 metres long. But this is small compared to its giant relative, as you can see from this picture of their **vertebrae** side by side.

The **Bluff Downs Giant Python** was named after the area where the fossil bones were found, Bluff Downs Station in northern Queensland. Backbones, teeth and ribs were found in 1992 alongside many bones of other prehistoric animals. All the fossil bones were well **preserved** in mud that would have been at the bottom of an ancient lake. Animals became trapped in the sticky mud and died there. Four million years ago, in the early Pliocene, the Bluff Downs area was **tropical** wetlands. This monster snake would have been common. At about 10 metres long and as round as a dinner plate, it is among the largest snakes known worldwide. The Bluff Downs python lived alongside other **megafauna** that would have been its prey, including wombats and their relatives.

Big Snake, Big Dinner

Pythons, like all reptiles, rely on the sun's energy to warm themselves up so they can be active and hunt for their next victim. The **Bluff Downs Giant Python** would have had no trouble catching large prey, wrapping its many coils around it and squeezing it to death. Then it would dislocate its lower jaw and slowly swallow its prey whole. When finished it would do nothing more than lie along a big tree branch while digesting its meal. This could take a long time, especially if it was big meal.

This modern-day python devours its prey just as its ancient relative would have done.

A Different Snake

The giant ***Wonambi naracoortensis*** (say wo-nam-bi nara-coort-ensis) was different from most snakes in that it could not dislocate its jaws. So it could only eat small to medium-sized animals, or eggs of birds such as mihirungs. Although smaller than the Bluff Downs Giant Python, it was still about 5 metres long, with a small head. *Wonambi* evolved from a Gondwanan ancestor that lived about 90 million years ago. This family once lived all over the world but became extinct millions of years ago. In Australia it existed until the arrival of humans with dogs, and probably its final territory was at Naracoorte in South Australia, where this fossil came from. It was the first prehistoric fossil snake to be described in Australia. *Wonambi* was the Aboriginal name for giant rainbow serpents that were said to inhabit sacred waterholes and enforce sacred law.

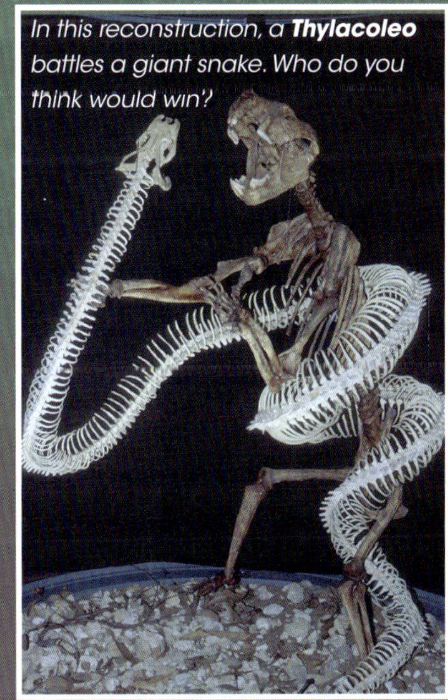
In this reconstruction, a ***Thylacoleo*** *battles a giant snake. Who do you think would win?*

Digging up Time

How do we know that life in our past actually existed? The evidence is in the rocks and soil and we can dig it up. For many hundreds of years, people have dug **fossils** out of the ground that have been lying there for millions of years. How do they get there?

A Lost World

Without fossils we would not have any idea about our **prehistoric** past at all. We would have a poorer understanding of our world. We would not know about dinosaurs, **diprotodons** or any of the other life forms of the prehistoric world. Fossils provide a window to anywhere in our past, from millions and millions of years ago to the last tens of thousands of years ago. Fossil bones are what scientists use to recreate accurate pictures of life then, and how it has **evolved** through time.

***Palaeontolgists** at Baldina creek, Redbanks Reserve, South Australia, examine fossils. This is a relatively young fossil site, with fossils about 60 000 to 100 000 years old.*

*Impression in sandstone of the **Ediacaran** animal **Dickinsonia**, about 600 million years old.*

Embedded in Time

When an animal dies it eventually disappears by being eaten or rotting away. But sometimes bones or teeth get preserved as fossils. The word fossil comes from the Latin *fossilis*, meaning it was dug up. Fossils may be preserved for thousands or even millions of years in sedimentary rock. Only a tiny number of the countless billions of living things that once lived on Earth are preserved as fossils. Fossils range in size from bones of huge dinosaurs to those of small bats. Special conditions are needed to preserve an animal's parts to make a fossil that will remain for all time.

From Live Animal to Fossil

Sedimentary rocks contain important information about the **prehistory** of the Earth. They are made up of layers upon layers of sediment. These are built up from little bits of our Earth that are washed into rivers and streams and end up on the bottom of a swamp, lake or sea. Here, animal and plant remains can be covered by layers of sediment. Fossilisation happens because the thick layers of sediment are compressed over a long time and turned to rock. **Erosion** slowly wears away the ground and eventually the layer with the **fossils** comes closer to the surface, where someone might dig it up.

An animal falls into a waterhole.

It decomposes or is eaten by other animals. Its bones get buried in mud on the floor of the waterhole.

Eventually the waterhole is filled up with layers of silt. Bones may later be exposed by erosion.

Layers of silt or sediment eventually become the rock in which palaeontologists search for fossils.

Unearthing Treasure

It is rare that a whole animal is preserved as a **fossil**. Usually it is a few bones, the claws, a tooth, or some teeth in a jaw. To be studied, fossils have to be extracted from the hard rock in which they were found. The rocks containing fossils may now be in mountains or in dry, dusty deserts—very different from the swamps, lakes, rivers or even oceans where they first formed. But whatever the fossil remains are, these treasures can tell an amazing story of life long ago.

*This fossil leg bone of the large prehistoric flightless **mihirung** bird is embedded in rock at Riversleigh World Heritage Area. Alongside the leg bone you can also see the gizzard stones that would help the animal grind up its food.*

***Thylacoleo** skull from a cave near Naracoorte, South Australia.*

*This articulated skeleton of **Thylacoleo** is in Fossil Cave at Naracoorte, South Australia.*

Important Special Sites

Riversleigh (Queensland) and Naracoorte (South Australia) are two important areas for fossil sites. Together they provide a fantastic record of the history of life on the land over the last 25 million years. They have been recognised as World Heritage Sites. Many of the animals in this book have been found there.

Found Where They Died

Sometimes bones are found on the floor of a cave where they have lain for thousands of years. Such fossils may be just about complete, looking like the animal has just lain down and died. But usually, unless the animal is covered quickly, other animals will walk all over it, or eat it, and the remains will usually be disarticulated and incomplete.

Mammal bones on the floor of a cave at Mt Cripps in Tasmania.

Caves

In caves the fossil-making process happens over a shorter period of time. Animals may fall into a cave and die. When sediment is washed into the cave, the bones are buried and become fossils. **Palaeontologists** can dig into the sediment in the cave and find bones that were deposited in only the last few thousands of years, or (rarely) up to about 1 million years ago. Most caves are usually totally destroyed by erosion of the land within about 1 million years, but in very lucky circumstances for a palaeontologist, the whole sediment contents of a cave (dirt and fossils) may become fossilised. Millions of years later, erosion may expose the ancient cave sediment (now rock) as the surrounding limestone rock is worn away. Australia has one of the most important sites where this has happened. Riversleigh World Heritage Area (Queensland) is renowned for its fantastic cave fills up to 25 million years old, which have fantastic fossils of many kinds of animals **preserved** in them.

Fossil Detectives

Scientists who study **fossils** are called **palaeontologists**. The word comes from Greek and means 'study of ancient life'. Finding fossils is a difficult job. Palaeontologists do not possess super-fossil-finding powers that cause fossils to magically appear to them and not to you. They have learnt to study clues that lead them to the fossils. They are really detectives. The smallest clue may be important.

Putting Meat on the Bones

Palaeontologists can rebuild an animal to see what it looked like alive. It's like putting together a jigsaw puzzle. Even though some pieces may be missing, palaeontologists can still work out the whole picture—the shape, size and 'look' of the animal. More bones give a more complete picture, by comparing them to other animal bones. But each bone has 'signs' that tell palaeontologists what group it is from—fish, **amphibian**, **reptile**, bird, or **mammal**—what type of animal and even what species. For example, if it was from a reptile, was it a dinosaur, or a lizard? If from a mammal, was it a **diprotodon** or a kangaroo? And lastly, smaller features tell them what species of animal it is. It may be one that has never been seen before.

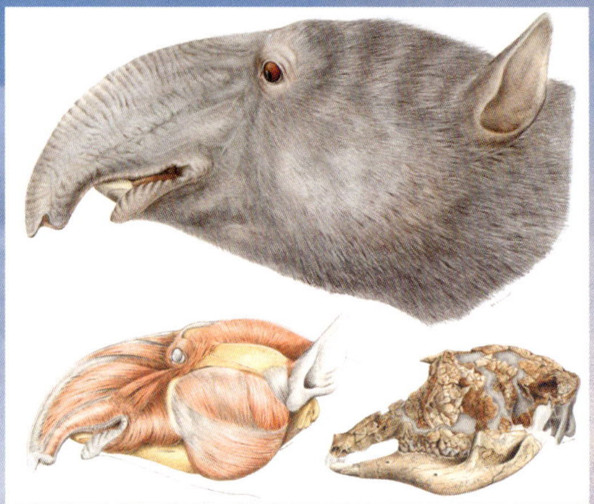

It's a Thingodonta!

Some fossil finds can stump the experts. They do not fit into the known groups or species. Until palaeontologists find new, more complete specimens these fossils remain a mystery. Name tags such as 'Thingodonta' and 'Bizarradonta' are wonderful reminders of the weird animals still being discovered. Surprises like these may turn up every time a palaeontologist goes out in the field digging.

Exciting, Dirty Work

In museums, palaeontologists can study a fossil, and tell if it's worth further investigating the site it came from. Digging for fossils is long, hard, dirty work. But it's exciting to be the first person to dig up and hold a bone of an animal that may have died 200 million years ago. And discovering the weird ways an animal was adapted to the world can reveal many surprises.

Lost in Time

As you read about the animals that have lived in Australia, you can see that life has changed slowly over millions and millions of years. Each of the animals was wonderfully adapted to its environment, but as the **habitats** changed, the animals had to adapt or go **extinct**. This has always occurred, even long before humans became good at speeding up **extinctions**.

Riversleigh, Queensland, a limestone hill where much of the fossil record of Australia is preserved.

Slow Changes

For millions of years animals expanded and lived throughout the land that is now Australia. The country was green and lush and **amphibians**, **reptiles**, birds and **mammals** thrived alongside countless millions of **invertebrates** such as spiders and insects. Over the last 15 million years the continent has slowly dried out. Now there is less rainforest and more desert. Yet the animals could adapt as the changes were slow.

Fast Change

About 50 000–40 000 years ago there was a fast change that caused the giant animals to go **extinct** rapidly. Some scientists think their disappearance is related to climate change. Others think humans caused it. Humans arrived in Australia about this time and their rock art shows that they encountered **megafauna**. Elsewhere in the world big animals went extinct when they met with people: people burnt the vegetation and ate the animals. Still others think it could have been a combination of the impact of humans and climate change. We need more evidence before we will know the answer for sure.

Sinco humans arrivod in Australia, chango has been faster. Humans painted some of the animals around them at the time.

SOS—Save Our Species

Our past is like a gigantic jigsaw puzzle with pieces missing. Scientists have been finding the answers to questions—missing pieces to complete the puzzle of our **prehistoric** life. Their discoveries about changes in animal populations through time also help with the conservation of **species** today. But there are still pieces missing. It will be up to future scientists to finish the puzzle and show us the complete picture. You may be the first person to dig up the bones of a completely new species that once lived here! And your research might help save some of today's unique Australian animals, such as the **Yellow-footed Rock Wallaby** (pictured) or Emu, from **extinction**.

Activities

The Prehistoric Animals of Australia Quiz

1. How do we know life in our past existed? (pages 8-9)
2. What are two important fossil sites in Australia? (pages 10–11)
3. A scientist who studies fossils is called what? (pages 12–13)
4. What word means to change slowly over time? (pages 14–15)
5. Why do animals move? (pages 16-17)
6. What does the word 'dinosaur' mean? (pages 18–19)
7. What is the most complete Aussie dinosaur to be discovered? (pages 20–21)
8. Name two Australian dinosaurs. (pages 22–23)
9. Birds of today came from what? (pages 24–25)
10. What are the five **vertebrate** groups of animals? (pages 26–27)
11. What are the three sorts of mammals? (pages 28–29)
12. What does the word 'diprotodon' mean? (pages 30–31)
13. Where did the Koala's ancestor live? (pages 32–33)
14. What were the weapons on the front feet of *Thylacoleo*? (pages 34–35)
15. Thylacoleo has teeth that could do what? (pages 34–35)
16. What finally cause the thylacine to become **extinct**? (pages 34–35)
17. What was the largest bird ever to have lived? (pages 36–37)
18. What was the largest lizard since the dinosaurs? (pages 38–39)
19. Name two unusual features of *Ninjemys*. (pages 40–41)
20. What is the one group of animals that has caused **extinctions**? (pages 42–43)

Glossary

Adapt	To alter behaviour to fit new conditions.
Amphibian	**Vertebrate** (backboned) animals that live on land but return to the water to breed. Frogs are amphibians.
Browsing/browsers	Animals that move around eating leaves and branches of plants. **Diprotodons** were browsing animals.
Carnivores	Animals that feed on other animals. Thylacines were carnivores.
Cretaceous period	The third time period of the **Mesozoic** era.
Diprotodon	The largest **marsupial** animal, and a cousin of today's wombat.
Dominant	When an animal rules all other animals. Dinosaurs were dominant reptiles.
Ediacaran	The earliest multicelled life on Earth, first found in the Flinders Ranges, South Australia. It also refers to the Ediacaran Period, approximately 635 to 542 million years ago, from which these animals come. It was named after the Edicara Hills.
Embryo	The unborn young inside the mother.
Endemic	A species is said to be endemic to an area, which could be a country or a place within a country, if it is found only there and nowhere else.
Erosion	When land is worn away by wind and water.
Evolve/evolution	Slow change from one thing into another. A species of dinosaur **evolved** into birds.
Extinct/extinction	When all the members of a group or species have died.
Fauna	Animals.
Fossils	The remains of living things that are **preserved** long after the plant or animal dies.
Gills	The breathing structures of fish and some amphibians.
Gondwana	The ancient land mass in the Southern Hemisphere.
Habitat	The environment where an animal species lives.
Herbivores	Animals that eat only plants. **Diprotodons** were herbivores.
Ichthyosaurs	Extinct reptiles that lived in the sea.
Invertebrates	Animals without backbones, such as snails and spiders.
Jurassic period	The second time period in the **Mesozoic** era.
Mammals	A group of animals that feed their offspring on milk from their own teats.
Marsupials	Mammals that develop their young in a pouch.
Megafauna	Big animals.
Mesozoic era	The middle era of the fossil record dominated by reptiles. (we may not need this when we have the time line)
Monotremes	**Mammals** that lay eggs. Only two types survive today: Platypus and two species of echidna.
Mosasaurs	Prehistoric lizards that lived in the sea.
Nocturnal	Active at night.
Omnivores	Animals that eat both plants and meat.
Ornithopods	Dinosaurs that moved about on their two back limbs, e.g. iguanodonts.
Palaeontologist	Scientist who studies fossils.

Placentals	**Mammals** that develop their young inside their body.
Plesiosaurs	Marine reptiles at the time of the dinosaurs.
Pleistocene epoch	The first epoch of the Quaternary period, during which there were many ice ages, separated by warm periods like the one we live in.
Predators/predation	Animals that kill other animals for food; the act of hunting and killing for food.
Prehistoric/prehistory	The period before recorded history.
Preserved	When the remains of once-living things survive in the earth.
Pterodactyls	Reptiles that could fly.
Reptiles	A class of cold-blooded animals with scaly skin.
Scavengers	Animals that feed off already dead animals.
Scutes	The bony coverings on some reptiles.
Sediment/sedimentary	Layers of soil, sand and other materials that get compressed and harden into rock. **Fossils** are found in sedimentary rocks.
Species	Animals that can breed with each other and have young. For example, a Saltwater Crocodile is a species of crocodile; a Freshwater Crocodile is a different species.
Tertiary period	The first time period after the dinosaurs when **mammals** ruled.
Triassic period	The oldest of the three periods of the Mesozoic era.
Tropical	Hot, wet and humid environments.
Vegetarians	Animals that eat only plants for food.
Vertebrae	The series of bones that make up the spine (backbone) of **vertebrate** animals.
Vertebrates	Animals with backbones.

Quiz Answers

1. Fossils
2. Riversleigh/Naracoorte
3. Palaeontologist
4. Evolve
5. To find food
6. Terrible lizard
7. 'Minmi'; an ankylosaur
8. Iguanodonts/Theropods
9. Archaeopteryx
10. Fish, **amphibian**, reptiles, birds and mammals
11. Monotremes, marsupials & placentals
12. Two front teeth
13. On the ground
14. A large claw
15. Stab & slice
16. They were hunted by humans
17. Mihirungs
18. Megalania
19. Horns and club tail
20. Humans

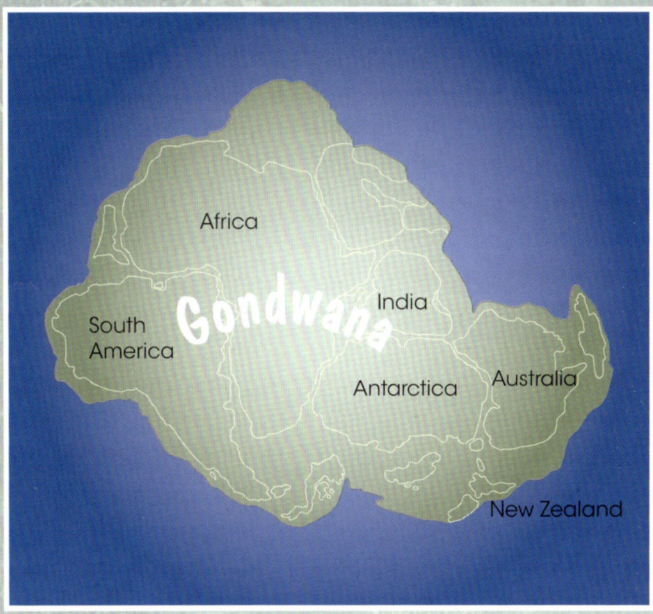

This is the Gondwana map from page 6, showing how it broke up into the different continents we know today.

What's in a Name?

The common names of animals are not always the same. That's why they have a two-part name in Latin called a scientific name—the scientific name of the marsupial lion is *Thylacoleo carnifex*. Scientific names are usually shown in italics, or somehow distinguished from other text. You can use the scientific names to look up the animals in other books and on websites.

Index